Burning Inside

An entrepreneur's guide to reaching your full potential in life and business.

Published by Timothy E. Borthwick
ISBN 978-0-359-80847-2

Dedicated to all those criticized for following their passion and sacrificing today so tomorrow they can live their dreams.

I also dedicate this book to my mother and sisters for their caring support and believing in me when I didn't believe in myself.

Be grateful, be loving, and support those who support positivity. It is the only way we will see the change we seek in the world.

Contents

*INTRO*DUCTION
Chapter 1

So you want to be an entrepreneur? You think you

have what it takes to build your own business

while getting hit with rejection, negative input from

friends or family and all the other shit that comes

with it? How late can your car payments go before

you give up? For how long can you go without

drinking with your friends on Friday or Saturday

nights because you're broke and chose to chase

your dream rather than chasing a good time. If

you're the person saying you can balance both

then you're full of shit or you're weak and you should put this book down. Someone who chooses to build something greater than themselves won't say that can balance both. You need to go all in if you want this bad enough. If you can't do that put this book down because I am wasting your time. Sorry, but that's just the reality to this game.

I just hit you with a small jab. I really hope most of you put the book down by now because it's only going to get more harsh and more real. So who am I and why am I writing all this shit?

It's simple, I care about people. I want to help people see the greatness inside themselves but it comes with a cleanse and a punch in the face with what's real and what you been taught your entire life. I was born in 1990 and what I can tell you is millennials are weak. We scare quickly and have trouble with criticism and understanding how things are. But also our parents are weak because that's the generation who trained us to feel and act this way. It's not a bad thing. Let's use it as a lesson and train ourselves to act and do differently. I am saying this to you because when times get hard and you feel like giving up, it is going to be the people willing to battle the criticism, rejection, pain and tragedy we face everyday in business and in life.

Here's another thing that might be hard for you to hear, no one cares about you, your business or your idea. Sucks to hear right? Well here's the truth of that. If no one knows you or your business and you provide them no value no one will care if you or your business exists. I don't mean your mom and dad here, I mean the people who will buy your shit and fill your pockets with cash.

I graduated college thinking the world was mine for the taking and I could be anything that I wanted to be. I had all these ideas and dreams and wanted to walk into a company making $100,000 a year and win the game of life. The market told me differently. When I graduated the market told me I could make $30,000 a year and sit at a comfy cubicle hanging pictures of my dog. I started getting hit so hard with reality and rejection that I thought life was over for me. I became depressed and did everything I could to learn to settle and be content. Family and friends told me, "Just be happy you have a job". I did everything I could to accept this as my reality but there was just something burning inside of me. I needed to show the world what I could do and I couldn't accept being another number on a spreadsheet. If that's you and you can be happy with average then im so happy for you, but this isn't for you. If you wake up burning inside or stay up late thinking about how you can create an impact and want to build the life of your dreams then this book is for you.

I didn't write this to hurt anyone's feelings or offend anyone, so please don't take what I say the wrong way. I wrote this thinking about myself and what I would have wanted in a mentor or a book to read before I began my journey. I didn't have mentors or guidance when I first started, someone telling me that things will be hard and tips to get me along in the process. I had to go out and meet people and some were big assholes but I still took their advice and applied it. I've applied advice and information from people I strongly dislike and denied advice or guidance from people I respect greatly. You see, if broke people or people who gave up are giving you advice despite being a nice person, that advice has little value. When we dive into the chapter on building your circle I will go over this in more detail.

If I can leave you with anything of value in this chapter it would be to start thinking about negatives and rejection as a good thing. Rejection, criticism and failure are the building blocks for you to become the person you need to be while building the business you desire. Failure or pain are only the end results if you allow them to be. Entrepreneurship is filled with this. You may feel it for 30 years, but a true entrepreneur will always lay everything on the line and fight through it no matter how long.

I come from a place of experience and much of what I cover many of you are facing or will face. Embrace it! Accept it and say BRING IT ON! It is all inevitable but within these chapters I will help you figure out how you can organize it, control it, and even combat it. When you accepted the responsibility of entrepreneurship you invited all of these problems and lows into your life. But what I will tell you is the end result, the light at the end of the tunnel makes it all worth it.

Let's dive right into the first exercise. This is something that you can apply to yourself and your business so let's do it for both. Think long and hard and answer the questions to your best ability.

Remember answering these will only help your

own growth.

Exercise 1

Describe in detail the last time you were

criticized for something you did or said.

_____

_____

_____

_____

_____

_____

_____

_____

_____

_____

_____

_____

**Describe in detail a time you were criticized,
judged or offended and it kept you from doing
something.**

_____

_____

_____

_____

_____

_____

_____

_____

_____

_____

_____

_____

_____

_____

**Describe in detail a time someone criticized
your business idea and list all the things that
person said as to why it wouldn't work.**

_____

_____

_____

_____

_____

_____

_____

_____

_____

_____

Use this blank area for additional notes.

SELF *AWARENESS*
Chapter 2

This is probably the most important chapter and I
made it the topic of chapter 2 on purpose. Self
awareness is one of the most lacking qualities of
human beings. If someone calls you an asshole
and you get angry at them without first identifying
why they might be calling you that then you could
be an asshole. If people label you as arrogant,
sexist or bias and you get angry before trying to
identify why they feel that way then you lack self
awareness. Criticism is a healthy tool to identify
areas you are lacking and can be a guideline to
help you change and become better. Now please

understand not all criticism is true but rejecting all criticism will not help you become who you want to be and who you should be.

Let's say you have customers who come into your coffee shop and leave suggestions in the suggestion box. You anticipate they will all be positive, but after reading them you find out your bathrooms are dirty, your coffee tastes bad and your bagels are hard as a rock. People will do one of two things. They will either get angry and change nothing or accept the criticism as an opportunity to be better. The second option will have a better result and you could end up being the best coffee shop in town because you were willing to improve rather than see it as a negative.

I hated criticism and avoided it at all costs. If you offended me I wouldn't talk to you. If someone criticized me I would become angry and hold a grudge and do nothing to improve. Accepting criticism is the first major step forward to becoming self aware. Embrace the criticism and identify it then figure out how you can fix it. Look at yourself in the mirror. Are you happy with what you see or have you been accepting the fact that mommy and daddy have been telling you that you're handsome or beautiful? Maybe you do need to get into the gym and make a change. Maybe you need to lay off of the soda and junk food because it's causing acne and your self image is the reason you don't get out of bed and get after your goals.

Perhaps you meet someone who has 50 years experience in business and they tell you to try XYZ and you're still doing ABC and you think they don't know what they're talking about then maybe you have an ego problem and it's time to work on that. Are you struggling to find the money to grow your business but somehow find the money to go out 2-3 times a week and buy new shoes, watches or clothes? You might have a spending problem or priority problem that you need to evaluate. Are you struggling to find time to work on yourself or your business but sleep through the alarm or spend 3-4 hours a day in front of the TV? You might have a time management problem or again your priorities are out of whack. Address the issue and identify the fact that you're the problem and you have the power to change it. You see, too many people want to blame the world, family, strangers or their jobs on why they can't do something and the reality is that 99% of the time it's because of you and you can't blame you.

So what are some things that you can do to become comfortable with self awareness and allowing yourself to identify the problems that you're creating. For me I started writing down what I didn't like about myself and some things I wanted to be better at. Here is how I set it up.

I want to have more time...

Things preventing me from having more time

1.   TV/internet

2.   To much sleep

3.   Too much leisure time

4.   Not writing down a schedule

5.   Not sticking to a schedule

I would set it up in a way similar to this and only list things that I was in full control of. If you have children then you need to create a schedule that fits everything in while still being able to care for your children, but if you are spending 2 hours of your child's nap watching reality TV then you are to blame and you can't use the fact that you have a child as the reason you can't achieve your goals. Watching reality TV wasn't the priority, your child and your business should be the priority.

Let's say you work 7am to 4pm and after work you have to be home to care for a relative but you want to get in shape. Your gym is on the way to work and you could get up at 5am, workout for 30-40 minutes and still make it to work on time but you continue to hit snooze because you love sleep then you can't blame anyone but you. You have the ability to get up and get to the gym no matter the circumstances yet you choose not to. You will not achieve the goal you desire and its not because of your after work responsibility but because of your lack of discipline to get up in the morning and make the dream a reality.

If you are weak, learn to be stronger. If you are undisciplined, learn to be disciplined. Once you identify what it is you lack or what others identify figure out how to make the change. It could mean finding the right person to mentor you or listen to. Maybe a book to read or a lesson plan you can follow. You need to become disciplined and most of us lack this quality and its the number one thing that's going to create the entrepreneur inside of you. Don't avoid it, be self aware, identify your lacking areas and attack them.

Self awareness goes even deeper than being lazy or unmotivated. Do you have a positive or negative attitude? If you're always negative do you think you will be successful? I was always negative, always blaming my circumstances and found the downside to everything and anything I did. It was my biggest downfall and everyone would address it except for me. Finally I was able to take what others said, realize what they were saying was true because I could see it and began working on it. I would surround myself with positive people and ask what they did to be so positive, I changed my diet and spent more time doing physical activity. I wanted to be the person who could take a negative situation and flip it upside down. I was fed up with being the person I was and I knew that if I continued to be that person, nothing in my life would ever change.

Let's now think about morals and intentions. Do you have good intentions? Do you want to help or hurt people? Are you in it for money or passion? We can dive so deep into what things people are unaware of but the truth is that we all know what things we need to make ourselves aware of and that we need to change. Assholes know they are assholes but choose to be and they haven't addressed the problem with themselves to make the change. People who have an ego problem know they have an ego problem but refuse to change it, why? Well that means they might have to be wrong sometimes or let others be right. But at the end of the day they know they have a problem. Self awareness is choosing to step up to the plate and address the issues holding you back from becoming the next version of you. Accept responsibility for these things and make the necessary improvements. You will not get to the next level unless you do.

Exercise 2

Identify 10 things that you feel you need to be more self aware of.

1.

2.

3.

4.

5.

6.

7.

8.

9.

10.

Identify 10 things that other people think you should be more self aware of. *For this exercise allow them to be open and honest. It will only help you in the end.*

1.

2.

3.

4.

5.

6.

7.

8.

9.

10.

Compare the results. If Anyone had a matching answer as you, write it down and begin working on it immediately.

1.

2.

3.

4.

5.

6.

7.

8.

9.

10.

WHAT *IS AN ENTREPRENEUR*
Chapter 3

I'm not talking about the Instagram Entrepreneur

with the pictures in front of someone's

Lambhorgini flashing fake watches. That's the

false reality social media creates to get people interested in buying someones program that can create wealth for you overnight. That's the image of it all that makes it attractive and sexy. What the media doesn't show you is the behind the scenes. Wealthy entrepreneurs do have the fancy sports cars and the nice houses and there's no doubting that. But if all you want to do is take a picture in front of a sports car to create credibility so you scam someone into buying your program does not make you an entrepreneur.

So then what makes someone an entrepreneur. By definition it is "a person who organizes and operates a business or

businesses, taking on greater than normal financial risks in order to do so". All of this is true but what I will say is it goes much deeper than this. Do you organize and operate the business on all levels? Yes. Do you take on huge financial risk? Absolutely. Already I can tell you that most of the "online entrepreneurs" do not want to do either of these things. They want the image that all of this eventually allows you to have. You have to go through a process before you can pay cash for a Aventador.

How many entrepreneurs do you know? How much time do you spend studying them, spending time with them, or asking them questions. If you know some you should be trying to do these things a lot. When I first started my first business I was working 16 hours a day some days. My first year I worked every weekend and most holidays. If I posted that on social media it would get less likes than the Lambo, but that is the majority of what an entrepreneur does, especially in the beginning. Yes, you are in full control and you can take a day off if you want to but building a business takes time, persistence and dedication. Looking at it as an 8 hour work day and expecting success is nothing short of stupid. When you're building a business and building a client base, money is coming in and you're covering your overhead and hitting milestones and think it's time to lay off the gas and take a vacation then the business gods will punish you, I promise you that. You'll know what I mean when it happens, trust me.

An entrepreneur is self aware, disciplined, focused, hard working, humble, never satisfied, seeks positivity, focuses on solutions rather than dwell in problems, etc, etc, etc. This list can go on for miles. But a good entrepreneur is not chasing the dollar. They are constantly improving, practicing and evolving. With that comes money. When you increase value and find solutions money will find you. But the focus is on those initial things. When I was chasing money and my only focus was money my goals were small, my wallet was thin and I struggled. I was hungry but got tired and eventually failed because my only thought was money. I didn't find solutions, I wasn't focused on value and I didn't set large goals.

An entrepreneur is a dreamer with a purpose. It's one thing to dream its another to make dreams a reality. Entrepreneurs see it before they understand how to create it. They don't think about what is impossible they see the front of the puzzle box and start adding pieces.

Please, DO NOT get caught in the social media entrepreneur. There is limited value there. You need to study real entrepreneurs that you meet at networking events, in books, the ones you see on stage in front of 30,000 people and not the ones posting in a mansion in the Hills that you can rent for $800 a day. Focus on real people building real businesses. I got so caught up in the online gurus. I honestly don't regret buying their programs because it was an investment in myself and it taught me who I didn't want to be. It was worth every penny.

An entrepreneur is a worker. You are not limited to average. You choose to stand out rather than fit in. You're not worried about having large groups of friends or whose doing what on Saturday nights.

You're not worried about where everyone else is in their lives. You found exactly what it is you want to do. You are pursuing the dream of building, creating and providing. You want to create jobs rather than hold a job. You want to lead people rather than follow. You see people as valuable. You focus on solutions rather than problems. You never give up and you never stop trying. If you feel these ideas inside of you than you might just be an entrepreneur.

Exercise 3

List all of the things that make you different from the people in your life, including friends and family.

_____

_____

_____

_____

_____

_____

_____

_____

_____

_____

_____

_____

Why do you think you have what it takes to be an entrepreneur?

_____

_____

_____

_____

_____

_____

_____

_____

_____

_____

_____

_____

List the top 5 entrepreneurs you follow and

one attribute you like about them.

_____

_____

_____

_____

_____

_____

_____

_____

START *WITH VALUE*

Chapter 4

Why do you buy something from a particular

brand? Why did you choose a certain gym? A

certain grocery store? A particular watch? You use

or purchased these things because you like them

but when you go a little deeper they provide some

sort of value for you. Convenience, customer

service, warranty, and price are all in the category

of value at some level for you the individual. These

companies understand the importance of value

and use that as a way to attract customers and

keep them. Now thats on a business level and we

will expand on this.

But I want you to think about the value that you

provide. What do you bring to the table? The

friends you attract or people you attract into your

life continue to show up because of something that you are providing. Maybe you're a good friend, you make them laugh, or maybe they're using you for money or the party's you throw. I want you to start thinking about the value that you bring to your life and other people's lives.

Right now, think about what value those people are bringing into your life. Do they push you to be better or tell you to slow down, take it easy, or what are you doing that for? Can you depend on them to be there for you? What are they providing for you? If you can't think of anything then it's time for those people to go. If you're surrounded by value lacking people then your value will never reach the right people. The less time you spend with people who lack value they more time you'll have for people who you can transfer value with.

You will then live a life of value and your focus will always be about providing value.

I had a large group of friends, so I thought. I had all these people who showed up for parties at my place and the fun I created for them. When I lost everything those same people stopped showing up. The phone stopped ringing and the people who I thought were there for me all went away. This happening multiple times in my life. Here is the value we were transferring, they were filling space in my home at my parties and I was providing them the party. Big picture, there was no value for me. I was being used and ultimately using them to fill space and avoid loneliness.

Another example, My first business partners. We would meet, I would provide the projects, the clients, the vision, goals, and the process. They did none of those things and chose to do the bare minimum. Simply put, I chose the wrong business partners. I was surrounding myself with value lacking individuals and it was driving my potential into the ground.

Understand this, surround yourself with value driven people who provide enormous amounts of value and in return provide value to them and to your customers. Next time you're at a networking event or meeting and you're engaging with someone new, find out what they bring to the table. Present to them what you bring to the table and find out if you can transfer value. You do that over and over until you're surrounded with people of value who appreciate the value you bring.

Now in order to do this you're going to have to provide value first. Find out what you can do for these people. Get them to understand you want to bring value to their lives and if they're value focused individuals they will return the value but you have to give before you can take so understand that. Too many times people want to receive before they give, don't be selfish.

In business when it comes to your customers or acquiring new customers value should always be the initial focus. If you focus on money you'll lack the value and limit your potential. Lead with value and you'll have an abundance. Focus on value in the content you create, the books you write, the stories you tell and the products you sell and you will reach your goals. Your customer wants to know they're getting what they pay for and need to trust you. If they feel they can't trust you or don't like you then they won't pay you it's very simple. If you start with value and the customer or prospect walk away with value but didn't buy but maybe give you a referral or answer a follow up call or buy something down the road then that's still a win for you. Listen to any top entrepreneur in the game right now they will all talk about value.

Here's the strategy for creating value in your life and your customers lives.

1.   Surround yourself with value focused individuals.

2.   Eliminate the value lacking individuals in your life.

3.   Lead with value before the sale.

4.   Provide value before asking for anything in return.

5.   Ask "what can I do for you".

6.   Become very familiar with what empathy means; Definition: The ability to understand and share the feelings of another.

7.   Study the value that people or businesses provide to you and enhance it.

8.   Think about what value is missing in the current situation.

Focus on these 8 points daily. These are all the things you can practice and become focused on daily. Entrepreneurs provide value. A solution is solving a problem with value in mind. Making things easier, better, faster, cheaper are value points to a consumer. When an entrepreneur gives a 2 hour presentation they are trying to provide information. Information is valuable. When an entrepreneur is first starting their business and going door to door explaining their product or service and demonstrating how it can help or change the prospects life or business and the prospect buys, then they saw the value in the salesperson and the product. Always lead with value. Always have value in mind. Value yourself and those you bring into your life. Value your product or service. Value your prospect or customer. Value people.

Exercise 4

List all the people who provide value in your life.

_____

_____

List all of the people in your life who lack value.

_____

_____

_____

_____

_____

_____

_____

_____

_____

_____

_____

_____

_____

_____

_____

List 5 to 10 things that you value as a

customer.

1.

2.

3.

4.

5.

6.

7.

8.

9.

10.

List 10 ways you can increase value in your life

right now.

1.

2.

3.

4.

5.

6.

7.

8.

9.

10.

GOAL *SETTING*

Chapter 5

Having goals is the number one thing that's going to get you to where you want to be. Setting big goals that both scare you and excite you is part of the recipe for achieving greatness. If your goal is to make $100,000 a year and live in a nice home you'll probably fall short and make $65,000 and live in a condo outside of the city. Something I've learned from listening to the great entrepreneurs of our time and my own experience is setting small goals leads to even smaller results. If you want to make $100,000 and buy a nice home then you better be setting million dollar goals and working hard as hell to attain it because if fall short of the goal you'll exceed your original expectations. You'll see exactly what it is you're capable of and probably end up setting up new goals to reach.

You should always be chasing goals. You should always have new goals. Crazy goals. Goals that would scare the person wanting $100,000 and a nice house. You should want to make a billion dollars and own real estate and not just a home. Small thinking will always lead to minimal results. Think big, dream big and go crazy.

Set your goals and write them down everyday until your goals are reached. All goals. If you want the fancy car right it down. Better yet write down that you want 10 of them. You'll fall short and maybe you'll end up with 3. 3 definitely exceeds the original thought of only having one. You want to build a 10 million dollar company then your goal should be a billion dollar company. See setting goals like this puts you in a position to think bigger and act bigger. You have to think and act a certain way to reach a billion dollars.

So step one is writing down your goals everyday. Big goals. Everyday until you reach that goal and replace it with a new goal. See, entrepreneurs are happy, excited and good people but they're never satisfied. They always want to get to the next level.

Step two is taking action on these goals. You need to figure out how to get after each goal to reach it. Don't overthink this part, just find one approach and get after it. Everyday figure out new ways of reaching the goal. Ask people, meet people who have what you want, who already reached this goal. Find out what they did and gather information so you can do what they did. You have to be resourceful in order to get to where you want to be. Sometimes that means becoming real humble and asking questions. Seeking people who laid the foundation and figuring out how they did it. You want the fancy car? Find people who have the fancy car and see how they did it. You want to own real estate? Hang out with investors and successful people in real estate. Set the goal and figure everything out once you've committed to that goal.

What are some of your goals? These can be personal goals or business goals. If you plan on playing small throw this book in the trash. If you want to break even or make enough to take the family on vacation once a year then you're playing small. You're training yourself to scrape by and play amongst the average people. I told you in the first chapter, this book is for people who want to go all in and win big. People who are absolutely obsessed with entrepreneurship and willing to do whatever it takes to be the big time entrepreneur they deserve to be. But if you want to play small and set small goals then the universe will punish you for that eventually and take everything. Business is cruel and when you sleep on success it will be taken away just as easy as it was to take your foot off the gas. Don't be weak.

Right now I want you to write down 10 of the biggest goals you can think of.

1.

2.

3.

4.

5.

6.

7.

8.

9.

10.

I bet most of you went conservative so now I want you to take the same goals and multiply every goal by 10.

1.

2.

3.

4.

5.

6.

7.

8.

9.

10.

How do your goals look now? Crazy?

Unimaginable? Out of reach? I bet they do and

that's exactly where you want to be. Here's why.

You will fall short of your goals and the work you

put in will never amount to the goal you set. That

is why you will fall short. If you want to make

$200,000 but you set a goal of $500,000 don't you

think you will have to work harder to reach the

goal of $500,000? You will have to meet more

people, speak to more prospects, work harder,

sleep less, and be more resourceful. If you fell

short and did $250,000, exceeding the original $200,000 but fell short of the $500,000 would you be happy? I would be but I most certainly wouldn't be satisfied. I would know what it takes to make a quarter of a million dollars and have an idea of what it would take to reach the $500,000.

Some goals you will never reach that's just reality hitting you again. It does not mean to don't pursue those goals everyday. What happens is new opportunity comes from chasing huge goals. You meet better people because your goals require you to connect with people to help you get there. This opens doors and creates new opportunities. Its real simple. Write down your goals and take action. Everyday

Exercise 5

Write down all of your goals again and list right beside it how you will take initial action to make that goal happen.

1.

2.

3.

4.

5.

6.

7.

8.

9.

10.

List your goals in order from most difficult to least difficult.

1.

2.

3.

4.

5.

6.

7.

8.

9.

10.

If you had only one year to make these goals a reality and had to start with the most difficult goal first how would you take action?

_____

_____

_____

_____

_____

_____

_____

_____

_____

_____

_____

_____

Create an action plan like this for all of your goals every single day and start looking at your goals like this. Goals are meaningless unless you take action.

PRACTICE *EVERYDAY*
AND ACCEPT FAILURE
Chapter 6

Both practice and failure go hand and hand.

Athletes, artists, musicians, and entrepreneurs

practice everyday and fail consistently in order to

reach the next level. If you think every amazing

athlete or billionaire woke and one day and started

winning championships or building fortune 500

companies without practice and failing then you

are delusional. The time you spend at perfecting

your craft and creating the opportunity to fail over

and over again are the bricks you lay everyday in

order to build the perfect house. The house being

you and your business. You will never have the

house. You will always have missing bricks, but

eventually you will lay enough bricks that it will

begin to look like a home.

The greatest athletes were not born great. You may have heard the saying "hard work beats talent" and it's true. The hard working athlete focuses on perfection and understands they will never be perfect but sets the goal to be perfect. The talented individual gets lost in their talent and might win one championship. Michael Jordan has six championships. He was cut from his high school team. Just remember that when you start to think about how much talent you lack. Get to work and work hard. Be perfect even though you will never be perfect.

Talent is a trap. Kids get praised for talent. I remember the talented athletes had exceptions and could be late, miss practice and had special privileges. Those kids lost the value of hard work and perseverance. Those kids are not athletes today. Those kids grew up to be a waste of talent and lack work ethic. Hard work will always beat talent. Again and again.

As an entrepreneur you are developing skills. You're perfecting a craft. You might not be a Picaso or a Jordan but you are still a craftsmen. Your profession is an art. It takes time to build it and eventually you can gain massive exposure and create a massive impact. Without practice everyday, multiple times a day and consistently for weeks, months and even years you will not become the mastering entrepreneur you desire to be.Failure is another important element. Many people avoid failure at all costs. They will shelter themselves from it, avoid humiliation, avoid looking stupid or becomign embarassed and all that does is prevent you from learning, growing and becoming comfortable with yourself and your pursuit of getting to where you want to be. Avoiding failure is detrimental to one's success. Avoiding it will only keep you from growing. Seek out the opportunity to fail and fail frequently. The amount you can learn from failing and how quickly you can learn from it is priceless. What you will learn about yourself and how much you can endure as well as how comfortable you will become is endless.

Go all in with failing. Do it quickly and consistently. It's going to be a valuable asset for you. I know this is hard to understand because growing up we were taught to avoid failure, avoid pain, avoid embarrassment. We have all been trained to stay away from failure. To become an entrepreneur you will have to fail over and over again. The reason is because what you're doing is so unique. A textbook or a test will not grant you access to success in business. You will have to learn the way through studying great people, practicing, failing and reapplying. Do not fear failing. For the future of your business and your own personal development fail as much as you can and reapply what it taught you.

Exercise 6

Why are you afraid of failing?

_____

_____

_____

_____

_____

_____

_____

_____

_____

_____

_____

Describe a time that you failed at something

but ended up learning something from it in the

process.

_____

_____

_____

_____

_____

_____

_____

_____

_____

_____

_____

_____

_____

List 5 things that you have failed at just this

year alone. List 5 things that you learned from

it.

1.

2.

3.

4.

5.

ELIMINATING FEAR
Chapter 7

What are you afraid of? What things do you allow

to enter your life and make you fearful?

Eliminating fear is extremely hard but at the same

it is an ongoing self improving process. Doing

what scares you over and over again puts you in a

position to eliminate that fear. If you fear public

speaking but put yourself in the position to speak

in front of crowds multiple times a month you are

then training your mind and body to become

comfortable in that situation. Fear usually comes

from lack of experience, training, self doubt, or lack of knowledge. By forcing yourself to do what scares you will ultimately train you to control or eliminate that fear.

Now I am not talking about fear of spiders or heights. But I am sure if you spent more time in high places or handling spiders that fear could also become more controllable or eliminated entirely. The fears I am mentioning in this chapter are the things that are holding you back from taking your life and business to the next level. If you fear you lack the knowledge then educate yourself. If you fear speaking in front of crowds but know that is the only way for people to become familiar with you and your products or services then you need to do just that and schedule speaking engagements and force yourself to face that fear. Speaking in front of people and to people is a major part of your entrepreneurial journey. By not doing so you will not reach the levels you wish to reach.

Now I know this is all easier said than done. I am telling you to do what scares you and not only do it once but do it over and over again until it becomes a part of your process rather than a burden in your life. The only way to become comfortable with your fears is through repetition and ongoing self improvement. I think about the first time I presented to a panel of angel investors as well as other entrepreneurs and spectators. I was beyond scared. I was petrified. But I knew I needed funding and I knew the only way for me to get to that next level was for me to do this. I needed investors and people to know me and my product.

I didn't want to do it, I hated every part of it and it wasn't until after I realized I only hated it because I've never done it. I never presented my product to people of that caliber, in front of that many people, in a setting where I had to pitch the way I did. It was an entirely new experience. After it was a huge relief. I did something so few are willing to do. I received a massive amount of feedback and interest in my product. I did not receive any initial funding but I instantly became hooked. I wanted to do it again because now I had the experience of already doing it. Now I wanted to perfect it. Who knew that this fear of mine that I made such a big deal about could be minimized so quickly. Now each time I pitch my business I gain more and more confidence. Speaking in front of larger crowds is becoming part of the process rather than a fear or burden limiting my success or abilities.

Don't get me wrong I am still nervous each time but once I begin my confidence excels the nerves every time. Preparation and repetition will always beat your fears. Right now I want to list some fears you could be facing in your own life and with your business and if I cover some of the ones you fear write these down for later, I'll begin.

- Public speaking
- Selling
- Hiring
- Interacting with new people or prospects
- Expansion
- What people think
- What friends or family think
- Losing money
- Getting sued

- Competition

These are just a few that some of you might fear that are more focused on your business but definitely are fears within you that you need to change. If you fear any of these I listed I can tell you it's because you're lacking the right guidance and information. Fear of losing money? Lack of knowledge or information. Fear of getting sued? Lack of information. Fear of selling? Lack of information. Your ability to prepare and your lack of knowledge has led you to fear what you don't know or have yet to experience. If you have experienced any of these things and failed then it comes down to lack of preparation and repetition. A batter is afraid of a 90 mile per hour fastball because they haven't hit a fastball going that fast, they haven't seen enough of them and they haven't hit enough of them.

You're afraid to stand in front of 500 people and pitch your idea because you haven't done it or you haven't done it enough. Do it over and over again. It's as simple as that.

How can you create repetition and gain knowledge to minimize fear?

- Networking events
- Speaking engagements
- Speaking to more strangers on a daily basis
- Pitching to businesses daily
- Practice speaking in front of the mirror

- Record videos and post them to youtube

- Read daily

- Seek mentoring daily

- Maximize your efforts and do these things

multiple times a day until you start minimizing fear.

There is no real secret here. All it comes down to
is doing an uncomfortable about what you fear
until you minimize the fear and do it over and over
again until it feels natural. Make it part of your
daily routine and constantly work on improving
your process and increasing your preparation.

Exercise 7

What are the top 10 things that you fear most?

1.

2.

3.

4.

5.

6.

7.

8.

9.

10.

What are the top five fears that you feel are holding you back the most?

1.

2.

3.

4.

5.

List 3 things you can do for each of your top 5 fears to help minimize the fear.

1.

-

-

-

2.

-

-

-

3.

-
-
-

4.

-
-
-

5.

-
-
-

Commit to working on these everyday. Once you do they will become part of your routine and second nature. Minimize your fears to start living to your true potential.

YOUR CIRCLE
Chapter 8

Who are the 5 people you spend the most time

with? What are they doing with their lives? What

are they doing to improve? How do they spend

their free time? These are important questions to

ask yourself because if you're spending all your

time with 5 losers than you will be number 6.

Surrounding yourself with undriven, unsuccessful,

and unmotivated people will be detrimental to your

success. The amount of people who will overlook

this chapter and not take my advice will be the

people who are in the same position next year.

Still broke and still wasting potential. People hate

this part because they know that the people they typically spend time with are losers. They know they shouldn't be spending time with these people and they want to avoid this topic entirely.

It's hard having to make a decision to cut people out so you can make room for value driven people. It's hard to say to a lifelong friend that you have to spend less time with them because your mission requires that you spend more time with people who act and think the way you do. Limiting time or cutting ties completely with the wrong people has always put me in a better situation. It has always allowed me to meet the right people and spend more time with those people once I made the decision to cut ties with the people who were not producing value in my life.

If you're trying to build a billion dollar a year business and create value for consumers and your employees do you really think you will get there by having your drunken idiot friends from high school still in your life? Do you think you'll become the next great speaker or build the next Facebook when you're partying with small minded people every weekend? You will stay the same if you choose to surround yourself with those people.

Now do I expect you to cut these people out of your life entirely. The answer is I wish you would but I can't expect you to do that. You care about these people, they have been a part of your life for a long time. What I need you to do in order to reach the level of success you desire is to shorten your time with them. Spend 90% of your time with big thinkers, people who you desire to be like or people who bring greater value to your life and business. Limit your time to 10% for those who are not adding the necessary amounts of value required for you to breakthrough and become the person you need to be.

What will happen when you begin to do this? You might lose these so called friends. They may become threatened by your success and who you're becoming. They will start to envy you rather than supporting you. You will hear people say that you have changed or you think you're better now that you started spending more time with successful people. If this is happening then you're doing exactly what you need to do. Trust me it's going to be hard at first to hear all this about you. But you know deep down that you're doing what's best for you and your family. To become the best version of yourself you must do what others are unwilling to do.

The best thing you can tell and friend or family member as to why you've become less present and you seem to be avoiding them is that your mission is requiring that you invest more time and energy in other places. You're not doing this to hurt anyone but in the end you will be the one hurting when you never reach your goals. Be selfish when it comes to your goals and one day it will allow you to be selfless.

Exercise 8

List all the people in your life that you need to start spending LESS time with.

1.

2.

3.

4.

5.

6.

7.

8.

9.

10.

11.

12.

13.

14.

15.

16.

17.

18.

19.

20.

If you have more than 20 people use a

notebook or writing pad to continue your list.

Write down all the reasons as to why you

should be spending LESS time with these

people.

_____

_____

_____

_____

_____

_____

LOW POINTS
Chapter 9

It's easy to feel defeated and feel like giving up in business. When you've been giving it your all and you feel like nothing is working, you feel like you're not good enough, unworthy, your competition is winning while you're losing, you lack motivation, you just feel like throwing in the towel. These low points in your journey can be painful. I get it. I've been there more than once. But what you do during these times will be the difference.

When you have no money, no customers and no desire to keep pushing that means it's time for you to kick it into overdrive. Close the computer, stop bashing your head against the wall or beating yourself up. The best thing you can do during these times is to get around people who have the energy, who are doing well or building momentum. See what they're doing and gather some insight and keep putting yourself around these people. Defeated people give up when it gets hard and sit around filling themselves with pity. A successful person who has hit some low points will get out there and fill themselves up with positive energy.

When ever I have felt beaten and defeated. When I have lacked ideas and can't seem to figure out how to get my business to generate an income or get to the next level I knew I needed two things. I needed an income and I needed to clear my mind. Sometimes when you're building your business and hit a wall that you can't get past you have to reset yourself. Get a part time job, surround yourself with other entrepreneurs who are hitting their high points and building success. When you take a step back for a little bit of time and spectate and become a student again many times you will figure out how to evolve and how to get back on track. Do not hurt yourself or your finances by sitting around feeling sorry for yourself. Put the business on hold and take a deep breath. Clear your mind and spend some time on something else.

Remember , it doesn't always happen right away for most of us. For most of us it can take years and years before we figure out our process. I had to fail 7 times and rejoin the workforce each and every time sucking up my pride in order to keep myself from becoming homeless and resetting my mind to discover what worked. I understand that it sucks to hit the low points in business. It sucks to have to have to put things on hold and get a job working for someone else. It sucks feeling small again. But you have to stay in control. Even if it means going back to work for some time you have to stay in control.

An entrepreneur does whatever it takes to stay on their path. Taking a job you hate that helps you stay on track financially or putting your business on hold to allow yourself to get your mind right are minor setbacks but not the end of your journey. For most of us it might just be part of the journey. It's a process and the process is much more than mansions and sports cars. Swallow your pride and take a step back during these low points and do what is necessary to keep going on the journey.

You can not allow yourself to feel defeated during these low points but you do have to be proactive during these times to make sure you stay on your path in all aspects. If you're unwilling to get a job when you struggle financially in your business than you are unwilling to do what it takes to keep your business. If you let pity take over rather than perseverance than you will trap yourself in weakness. Feeling weakness while feeling stuck is a recipe for disaster.

When I felt both of these things I fell into a long painful depression that felt impossible to escape. When you feel stuck keep kicking, keep fighting and keep moving forward even if its parallel to your goal. Please understand that these low points you face are some of the best things that will ever happen to you. They will teach you. They will make you stronger and they will shape you. If you can get through these hard times you can get through anything and one day you can then help others get through their lowest points.

Exercise 9

Describe the lowest you have felt this year or the past year and explain how you worked through it or how you were unable to work through it and allowed it to defeat you.

_____

_____

_____

_____

_____

List some low points that you could face and how you will combat them in order to continue pursuing your journey.

_____

_____

_____

_____

_____

_____

_____

_____

_____

_____

_____

HIGH POINTS
Chapter 10

Low points are not the only things that can defeat

you or put a stop to your growth or success.

Success and high points in your business and life

can slow things down for you or even destroy all

you have worked hard for. Now what do I mean by

this? Just because you have customers and your finances are in order does not mean you step off of the gas or slow down. It is not a time to take a break or spending most of your days on vacation. Falling asleep at the wheel of your business can easily derail you. People become so content in small doses of success that they think they have reached their full potential and end up losing everything.

When you reach your highs raise the bar. Remember you can be happy but you should never be satisfied. There are different levels of satisfaction and its a scale that you should always be trying to tip. When I became content with my business and stepped off the gas I lost everything. When I mentioned in earlier chapters about the business gods, sometimes it seems like there is a greater force that corrects you if you let up or take it easy. It's a big mistake and it should never happen. When you are winning in business work harder and set the bar even higher. It's in those times you should have the most energy and momentum.

It's very simple. When you're winning continue to win. Continue to improve and be hungrier than ever. It is not greedy as some might say. It's about securing your life and your business. There will come a day where you look back at these times and realize you made the right decision to keep the foot on the gas and grow your business by consistently raising the bar and never becoming satisfied. By doing so will allow you to live the life you've always wanted and help the people you want to help.

Exercise 10

Describe a time that you had reached a high point in your life or business and you let off of the gas and it caused you to go backwards rather than forward.

_____

_____

_____

_____

_____

_____

_____

_____

_____

_____

_____

_____

_____

_____

_____

List all of the ways that you think you can
avoid losing momentum during your high
points.

_____

_____

_____

_____

_____

_____

ALWAYS PITCHING
Chapter 11

You have this product or service, you want to

change the lives of the people you sell to and you

want to make a difference in the world. But how often are you pitching and selling the idea to your audience. I run into countless numbers of entrepreneurs who have these great ideas but I'll ask them, "So how often are you pitching your idea and how many people are you talking to on a daily basis?" Most will say the same thing, "I'm not" or "not as much as I should be". It's crazy to me. You want to be an entrepreneur, change lives, make an impact yet you never get in front of your audience. Most don't even know who their audience is. They're so caught up in the idea of their product or service that they don't even try selling it then wonder why they haven't made any money. How does your business have any value if no one is buying it or using it? How can you expand and get it into everyone's hands if you're not pitching.

Always be pitching everywhere. How else will you figure out who your audience is? You see in the beginning you can't always be hiding behind a computer running ads. People need to know who you are in real life and know you're a real person. People need to see the face behind the idea. They need to support you to support the idea of buying what it is you're selling. Where can you do this? Networking events, speaking gigs, chamber of commerce, meetups, blogs, video content, walking up to random people, the options are endless, but you need to always be pitching. Put your idea out there. Let people know about your products or services. Its practice and at the same time it's helping you figure out the need for what it is you're selling.

I'll pitch to everyone. I don't even care if they like me after I do it but it's allowing people to get to know who I am. I want to make a connection and expand my brand. I want to educate people and help them understand why they should buy from me. I want to be an expert in my field. Pitching is that preparation and repetition I was talking about. Now when I go places the people I've already pitched to are introducing me to other people. Its creating credibility and allowing other people to almost sell for me. I want people to introduce me to their friends or business partners as Tim the Founder of Company ABC where they do XYZ. Now I have people working as a spokesman for me. It's saving me time so I can go on to pitch to other people.

You absolutely need people to know you and know what you do in order to grow, expand and become massive. Yes not all people will like you or like your idea but that doesn't need to become a reason for you to never be doing it. If anything it should be the reason you do it more and more. Pitch to anyone and everyone. If they don't buy or are not the right prospect at least they know you and know what your business is all about. Somewhere down the line they will talk to someone about you who can use your product or service.

Exercise 11

Pitch to at least 10 people a day and write down exactly what happened after every pitch.

1.

2.

3.

4.

5.

6.

7.

8.

9.

10.

Continue to repeat this exercise everyday in a

separate journal or note pad.

After your first week add an additional 10

people per day per week.

Example

Week 2 - 20 people per day

Week 3- 30 people per day

Week 4- 40 people per day

And so on until the world knows who you are.

DOCUMENT EVERYTHING
Chapter 12

One thing you will hear most entrepreneurs say is that they wish they documented everything when they first started. They didn't capture the journey before the success and fame. Documenting everything you do and showing the world the process will do a few things for you. It will help build your audience, It will show people the real side of entrepreneurship wen starting and it will start to create a relationship with potential prospects. You see, everyone only wants to document the good shit and the cool stuff. They want to show the cars and the lifestyle but for me, I'm more attracted to the work and how the person started. I like the story and the journey. I could care less about how rich the person is. I want to see how they did it. The truth is much of your audience wants to see that as well.

How should you go about doing this? Grab your phone or camera and start documenting your daily process. People want to see the struggle and the process. Show the bills that you're behind on. Record yourself going to a networking event and why it's so important to attend. By doing this you will add value for your audience as well as teaching yourself how to become a teacher. Teach yourself to teach. Learn how to create valuable content. Enough pictures of the Ferrari when you're broke and haven't done shit. Instead record a video talking about how you're behind on all your bills and you're still pushing everyday. Follow that up with a video getting up at 5am and getting to work. Show people your process so they can learn from you. When people can learn from you they'll respect you. So one more time if you weren't paying attention. Document everything you do and start posting now.

Exercise 12

Record 5 pieces of content this week only covering your journey.

Video 1 - Who are you?

Video 2 - Why you started?

Video 3 - What has entrepreneurship taught you?

Video 4 - 5 things that you are struggling with.

Video 5 - Explain how your product or service can help your customers.

Video Guidelines

- **DO NOT focus on video quality**

- **FOCUS on value**

- **FOCUS on your ideal prospect**

- **FOCUS on helping the viewer**

- **ASK a question at the end of the video to allow your prospect to engage with you**

- **Use criticism as feedback to improve**

- **Don't worry about what others say about you**

- **Smile**

- **Thank your viewers**

- **On the 5th video create an offer of some kind or giveaway something for free**

- **Be passionate**

TRACK *YOUR PROGRESS*
Chapter 13

Have you ever started a diet or started a new

workout routine and you tracked everything you

did including progress you made? Could be losing

weight, moving up in weight or reps during your

workouts or even tracking your health. Tracking

your progress allows you to set the course of your

goals. You have to lose 5 pounds before you can lose 50 pounds but you need to know exactly how you lost 5 pounds so you can improve the diet and know what it took to accomplish the weight loss. Your progress as an entrepreneur should be the same way.

Now how should you do this and what should you track? The answer is to take a pencil and notebook and track everything. Did you go to the 25 networking events to said you would go to. Now it's sunday and you only went to 20 of them. Why didn't you go to all 25 of these meetings? What stopped you from going to all of them? Write down your goals and anything that prevented you from reaching them. The following week you may have completed all the tasks you set out to complete. You do this for 3 weeks straight.

What has changed in your business and life because of it? Maybe you met 5 people to add to your circle and now they're adding value that you can apply to your business. Maybe to turn 10 prospects into 10 paying customers and because you were tracking this you can clearly see what things you did in that time frame that helped you open these new doors for you. Do this over and over again and continue to track everything you do. Then once you have enough data you begin evaluating and figure out where the progress was made. What things did you do in order to make the progress and reach goals? Now take those things and enhance them. Do those things more frequently and at a greater volume.

Track daily routine + What things did you do to increase success (Track progress) = key factors in success

Repeat this formula and continue to improve and enhance it.

Exercise 13

Get yourself a journal or notebook to begin tracking your progress. Try this for 30 days by doing exactly what is listed below.

Write down 1 goal you want to reach.
Write down 5 things you can do to attain this goal.

Work at these 5 things every day for 30 days.

Double your efforts every week.

Track everything you do every day.

Track your daily results.

Evaluate your results at the end of 30 days.

If you missed a step and you did not have

successful results at the end of 30 days then

repeat this sequence until you find the desired

results. Remember is a journey that requires

discipline.

PUTTING IT ALL TOGETHER
Chapter 14

I hope some of you made it to the end here. I hope

I added value to your life that you can carry with

you. I'm sure I disappointed many of you because

you were looking for secrets or for someone to do

it all for you, some turn key solution. It doesn't

work that way, I wish it did. I want to try and put

everything together for you in this last chapter and

hopefully lay a solid blueprint that you can follow

everyday. I kept these chapters short and

eliminate the waste because I want you to get

going right away on all of this and start building

your future today. I don't want people spending a

month reading my book. I want people spending 4

hours reading it and begin applying everything I covered right away.

The Blueprint

I gave you an introduction to how started and laid the foundation of entrepreneurship. It's a journey and ongoing process. You don't just wake up one day a success. You sought out to build something and create financial freedom for yourself. There was something burning inside of you that you just had to pursue it. You made a decision to let the flame burn bright instead of doing what the average do and put the flame out. We all had a vision for our future and everyone has thought of financial freedom and dreaming of becoming something great. Very few choose to follow the path of true success and creation.

Being a true entrepreneur is never giving up. It's a constant push to become the better version of yourself. It's self awareness and deciding to be a lifelong student. An entrepreneur always focusing on perfection, knowing they will never be perfect. They provide solutions with a focus on value. They think about process improvements with both the customers and their employees in mind.

Everyday you should be setting goals and putting yourself in position to raise the bar. Doing what you fear because you know the results will help you create the life of your dreams. Practice everyday and accept your failures. Remember failing is the ultimate tool for success as an entrepreneur. It's the textbook that you write for yourself and failing is packed with learning material.

We talked about the highs and lows. I discussed how when times are bad you need to stay on course but take a step back. This could mean getting a job when finances are low or spending time studying successful people who are accomplishing their goals so you can restart your brain. Sometimes we just need to recharge and focus on different things to be able to see things a little clearer. When times are great, never ever take your foot off of the gas. Keep going, push harder and do more. If you let up and take a break you will be punished for it.

Document and track your progress on everything you do. Document your journey and not just the material things you gather along the way. Track your progress and find what things worked to create the success it brought you, then once you do enhance it and multiply your efforts. Last but not least remember to always be pitching yourself and your business. Make people know who you are or else no one will ever know who you are or what you can provide them. Provide value, seek people of value, expand your circle of successful people and limit the time you spend with negative people or to be frank, limit your time with losers.

Keep the fire burning inside of you everyday by following what I stated. If you decide to skip something or give an area less time because you find it useless or lack of interest in doing it then you're missing the most important part of entrepreneurship which is discipline. If you can be disciplined enough to do everything in this book then you can then work on scaling that to be disciplined in life and business.

I wish you all the best and my only hope in writing this book is to help create success in your life and be an impact. If I can help one person then I'm happy but I really hope to help so much more. Stick to the plan, work hard and be consistent in your efforts. Do not stop here, continue seeking knowledge and mentorship, surround yourself with successful people and you will find what it is you're looking for.

Exercise 14

What is at least one thing you learned after reading this book that you didn't know or understand before reading it?

_____

_____

_____

_____

_____

_____

_____

_____

_____

_____

Do you feel confident in your approach now that you have read this book? If not, what will you do next to feel that confidence?

_____

_____

_____

_____

_____

_____

_____

_____

_____

_____

_____

_____

List 5 things you want to take action on right now.

1.

2.

3.

4.

5.

How will you take action on these 5 things you listed?

1.

2.

3.

4.

5.

List one goal you can begin working on now and accomplish within the next 30 days. Explain to yourself exactly how you will reach this goal within the next 30 days with what you learned from reading.

GOAL:_____

___

HOW WILL I ACCOMPLISH

IT:_____

_____

_____

_____

_____

_____